Breadcrumbs From Heaven

Follow the trail of horses, faith,
and children with special needs to
Reins of Grace Therapeutic Riding Center

JULIA E. SAVITSKY

authorHOUSE

AuthorHouse™
1663 Liberty Drive
Bloomington, IN 47403
www.authorhouse.com
Phone: 1 (800) 839-8640

Published by AuthorHouse 02/27/2020

ISBN: 978-1-7283-4873-5 (sc)
ISBN: 978-1-7283-4872-8 (e)

Library of Congress Control Number: 2020903941

Print information available on the last page.

This book is printed on acid-free paper.

CONTENTS

DEDICATION PAGE

To my husband, Bob, who in this journey of faith and trust, gets the top prize. It's one thing to feel a personal calling from God but much more difficult to have faith in someone else's faith. I'm pretty sure he reviewed our wedding vows and in the "for better or worse" section *did not* find anything about moving to the country, mowing and weed-whacking acres of land, or battling 4' snow drifts down a 250' driveway to take the garbage to the curb. Everything about this journey has been out of Bob's comfort zone, but his faith in and dedication to our Lord and Savior, Jesus Christ, keeps him steadfast. *"I can do all things through Him who strengthens me" (Phil. 4.13).*

Reins of Grace Therapeutic Riding Center

ACKNOWLEDGEMENTS

I want to thank my family for putting up with me on this roller coaster journey and taking each step blindly, one at a time, fully relying on God even as they rolled their eyes a bit.

There are *so many* friends, co-workers, colleagues, volunteers, families, riders, and the Board of Directors—past and present—whom God has sent and will send to Reins of Grace. Each person who has crossed the barn threshold has made a mark on my heart and soul and taught me more than I've ever taught anyone in the arena. I thought I'd started out as a teacher, but as it turns out, I was the student of "Life, Love, and God 101."

And a *very special thanks* to Editor Extraordinaire, Deb Vessels. A casual conversation in the barn in the summer of 2019 was another nudge from God to write the book, when she said she could "help with editing," which was the understatement of the year. I had no idea the English language had so many rules—and Deb knows every single one of them.

Breadcrumbs from Heaven—what does that even mean? Is it an Old Testament reference to the manna God provided to the Israelites in the desert? Or the quail? Is it a new version of Hansel and Gretel on a religious retreat? *"Then the LORD said to Moses, 'I will rain down bread from heaven for you. The people are to go out each day and gather enough for that day. In this way I will test them and <u>see whether they will follow my instructions</u>'" (English Standard Version, Exod. 16.4).*

What best describes this story is the scripture verse about manna from heaven. God provided exactly what the Israelites needed in the correct amount. Of course, His timing was perfect; it came when they needed the nourishment and encouragement. He was *faithful* to His word and was *with* them. As with the Israelites, God provided everything we needed to build Reins of Grace Therapeutic Riding Center, one breadcrumb at a time. *"For I know the plans I have for you, declares the Lord, plans to prosper you and not harm you, plans to give you a hope and a future" (Jer. 29.11).*

This book will allow the reader a quick glimpse into the fascinating world of therapeutic riding and hippotherapy. A few brief chapters—Levi's Story, Becky's Story and Pearlie's Story—will let you see the incredible diversity, generosity, and willingness of our equine partners as they work with us and our precious riders. Their ability to *connect with us*—their human partners—and *recognize our needs* beyond our facades and physical boundaries is truly uncanny.

REINS OF GRACE
THERAPEUTIC RIDING CENTER

CHAPTER 1

Quit Horsin' Around and Write the Book

The morning of September 1, 2016, was spectacular. Not a cloud in the sky. Temperatures had dropped overnight, necessitating jeans instead of shorts. It was Thursday morning, and I had a big day of chores ahead of me. At about 7:20 a.m., the phone rang. I got a panicked call from my friend Sheri, saying that her mother-in-law, while driving her Westfield school bus route, saw a horse galloping down the road by our house. She knew we had horses and was worried that it was one of ours, running loose. Dashing out to the barn to count heads, thankfully, I found that all my girls were present and accounted for.

As I looked south towards 206th Street, sure enough, there was a lone horse galloping westward in the field. I immediately grabbed a halter and lead rope and ran into the house to get car keys. I jumped into my husband's SUV and set out to catch her and bring her back to our pastures until we could locate the owner. Heading west on 206th, I saw her, and she had slowed down in the field. I put the hazard lights on and called softly to her. Immediately, she stepped toward me. I was able to approach her, stroke her neck soothingly, and tell her what a good girl she was. She stood quietly as I put the halter on. I could tell by her condition that she had been well-cared-for, and somebody was probably desperately searching for her.

I tied her to a telephone pole briefly, so I could turn my car around to face east and head back to my house. I got in the car, rolled the window down, and began walking her back to our house. While I drove, she clip-clopped along beside me as I held the lead rope through the open window.

Looking eastward, I saw a big black truck coming toward us. Immediately, I stopped and pulled as far off the road as I could, although there was very little shoulder and a steep ditch. I put on my hazard lights, got out of the car, and walked the horse and myself around to stand behind my car for protection. I started flagging down the truck. The driver stopped alongside us and rolled down his window. "Do you recognize this horse?" I asked. He responded he wasn't a "horse guy" and had no idea where she might have come from.

At the same time, I became aware of movement in my peripheral vision. Looking west, I saw a red SUV in my lane, headed toward me. I started to wave my arms as a caution to the driver to slow down. Both lanes were completely blocked by the truck, my SUV, myself, and the horse—a *huge* visual roadblock.

I was able to wave my arm barely two times before the red SUV slammed into me and the horse, pinning us between her front bumper and the rear bumper of my car. Strangely enough, it didn't really hurt at that moment; it just felt like a lot of pressure. My immediate thought after the impact was that my endocrinologist, who continually told me I needed to take more calcium, was going to be unhappy because surely the bones in my leg must have turned to dust from the impact.

As I saw the horse running across the field, I thought *rats! We're going to have to go catch her again.* Deciding that it would be best to lie down for a moment, I felt myself doing so very carefully. I became aware of the driver who hit us as she stood by my head, saying, "I have no insurance and I have a baby in the car!" Her tone was accusatory as if it were my fault that she hadn't seen the roadblock. However, it dawned on me that all I had seen before impact was the top of a head; the driver was looking down.

I became aware that the driver of the truck was on the phone, but for some reason it didn't sound like he had called 911. So, with nothing better to do than lie there until help came, I decided that I had better do it. Before that, however, I called Bob and said, "I've been hit; come get me." Fortunately, I was so close to home that he could see the cluster of vehicles a mere quarter of a mile away.

I called 911, and from my CPR training, I knew to stay on the phone. I told the operator what had happened and just waited. Next thing I knew, I saw Bob approaching, and he had caught the horse. I cautioned him to stay back because I was afraid the horse would get spooked when the EMS team arrived, and I didn't want to get trampled.

I could see that the horse was bleeding steadily from a cut on her leg. I instructed Bob to take his shirt off and tie it around the horse's leg to help staunch the flow of blood. Next, I pulled up my veterinarian's phone number and gave the phone to Bob. The horse seemed better than expected; she had three cuts that I could see but seemed to be standing appropriately on all four legs. Relieved, I was trusting she didn't have any broken bones. However, there was no telling about internal injuries.

In all this time, I had not felt any significant pain but sensed only pressure and numbness. Additionally, I had not passed out. I think my natural bossiness, control-freak, take-charge nature asserted itself and distracted me from my injury. About that time, the EMS service team arrived and started doing their checks. As they asked about which parts of my body hurt, I told them just my leg.

The EMTs started their assessment at my head and worked their way down. By the time they got to my left lower leg, I heard them say we needed to go to the 86th Street hospital in Indianapolis. I didn't understand at the time why they would go so far when there were hospitals in Carmel and Noblesville that were much closer. Later, I found out why: the hospital on 86th Street is a level-one trauma-certified hospital, and the extent of the injury required such.

After they loaded me into the ambulance, they had to cut off my shirt and pants; I was especially distressed about my shirt as it was my new annual family-vacation shirt that I had just received a few weeks earlier. Interesting what is important after a healthy dose of trauma and adrenaline. It was about this time that the said adrenaline started to wear off, and I could feel my leg starting to throb.

They finally gave me some pain medicine, and things got a little fuzzy. When I woke up, I was in the hospital. My mom and dad, Bob, and my son Andrew were there, and Father Sean came in to bless me. No one told me the extent of my injury—but to see a priest already there was a little disturbing.

I pleaded with my family to take a picture so I could see and understand what was going on. It wasn't pretty. I had suffered a degloving injury to my left lower extremity, which simply means all the skin, subcutaneous tissue, and fat, right down to the muscle layer, had been twisted off between my knee and my ankle. After attempts to save the surrounding tissue, they had to remove all the flesh around my leg between my knee and ankle, including 70% of my calf musculature.

Miraculously, I suffered no broken bones and neither did the horse when we were hit. She had a couple of flesh wounds that my vet was able to stitch up, and within a few weeks, she was back to her regular job. There were no other injuries for either of us: no internal injuries, no pelvic fractures, no head injuries—simply unfathomable since the horse and I were hit at approximately 40 mph and smashed between the front bumper of the girl's SUV and the back bumper of mine.

On Monday, four days after the accident, I was transferred to the burn unit at Eskanazi in downtown Indianapolis for extensive skin grafting to cover the leg. The whole process of skin grafting was fascinating—maybe a little less so since it was my leg—but medically and scientifically, it's quite a process.

During the initial twenty-one days in the hospital, I had sixteen surgeries. At one point, the skin graft sites became infected, and I had to be hospitalized an additional ten days.

On October 5, 2016, a Sunday, I was able to attend Mass for the first time since the accident. Father Kevin saw us and welcomed back "our very own miracle." As we came out of church, we ran into Deacon Steve Miller. He said he had been praying for us but didn't know the details. I told him about the accident. When I got to the part where they found my shoes in *exactly* the same spot that I had been standing when I was hit (and not scattered across the road), I told him my guardian angels had lifted me up just in time to prevent any more damage and laid me down in the road.

Side note: A few years ago, I wanted to know the name of my guardian angel. I was told to pray before going to sleep and ask God, if He willed it, to reveal the name of my angel. In the morning, the first name that popped into my head would be my guardian angel's name. I had said that prayer and the next morning two names—Francis and Randy—popped into my head. Randy seemed a bit odd for an angel's name, but oh, well. I was a little confused; I didn't know if that was the first and last name, or if it was Francis-Randy, Randy-Francis (did angels hyphenate?), or if I had two angels. I told Bob that morning about the two names I heard. He replied that I must have two angels: one for the barn and one for everything else.

As I said, I told Deacon Steve that the day of the accident, my guardian angels lifted me up and out from between the two cars. He looked at me with a funny expression and asked if I knew what day it was. I thought to myself *it must be a trick question* since we had just come from Mass, but I dutifully replied, "It's Sunday." Steve said, "No, it's *Guardian Angel* Sunday." I was raised Catholic, but I had never heard of Guardian Angel Sunday. It is on the Church calendar, but it gets moved around.

During my ordeal, community involvement with prayer, meals, cards, and phone calls was overwhelmingly encouraging and uplifting. I know for a fact that by the grace of God and the prayers of the St. Maria Goretti community, I made a greater recovery than the doctors ever gave me hope for.

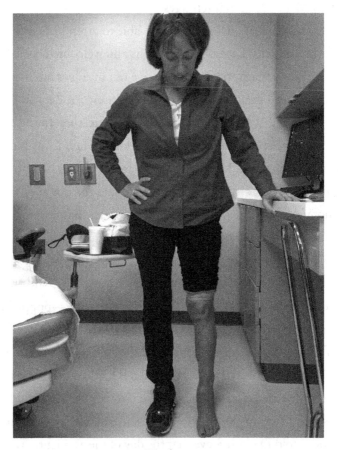

Healing

My friend Bill had pestered me for over two years to write the story of Reins of Grace. I was very reluctant since "I am writing a book" sounded too pretentious, and I am most definitely not a writer.

Since I was in for a lengthy recovery, I had an obvious opportunity to write the story of Reins of Grace, as Bill had encouraged me to do. So it was time to stop horsin' around and write this book.

Reins of Grace Therapeutic Riding Center was never on my radar. In other words, there was never any grand dream, never any blueprints or business plan, and never a "when I grow up, I'm going to have a therapeutic riding center." God, however, had planned this ministry from the beginning, and He planned this book to make sure it was shared with anyone who might benefit from it.

Follow this written journey from a determined, stubborn ten-year-old girl to the answered prayers of another ten-year-old girl—almost thirty years later. Eventually, Reins of Grace Therapeutic Riding Center was born; and then, following my faith-testing, catastrophic accident, so was this book. Watch and see how God was intimately, physically, and spiritually guiding each step of this remarkable journey. I didn't have to be Mother Teresa, a pastor, a nun, or even a very theologically-minded individual *to walk hand in hand with* God because God loves me—*and you*—completely, just the way we are, and wants to be involved in our *day to day lives*—every day, every thought, every activity. He gave me direction, instruction, and clues, one breadcrumb at a time.

Now, let's go back to the beginning, where it all started...

CHAPTER 2

Foreshadowing

Growing up in Kalamazoo, Michigan, I was one of four children, two boys and two girls, and as the second child and older girl, I was the oddball. My siblings dubbed me, "Ms. Mature." My interests were different than the rest of the family's. They all liked to play tennis, and even though I attempted to play tennis, my heart only had room for horses.

My first experience with horses was at the Kalamazoo County Fair. I had my first ride on a pony, chained to a large round metal wheel, and we simply walked in a circle for about ten minutes. However, that day, I was bitten by the "horse bug" and never looked back. I kept pestering my parents for a pony at every holiday, birthday, Christmas—any opportunity for a gift—and all I wanted was a pony. Repeatedly my parents told me that we couldn't afford a horse, nor could we afford to board it. With the wisdom and life experience of a soon-to-be ten-year-old, I thought to myself *if that's all that stands in the way of getting my pony, surely I can figure something out.*

I started saving every penny I could from babysitting, weeding the yard, emptying the dishwasher, and doing chores around the house.

Scouring the newspaper every week, I looked for my pony. About a mile away from our neighborhood lived a family whose daughter babysat for us, and they had horses on their land. I went to their house and arranged for board in exchange for labor, planning for that future day when I would buy my pony.

I finally saved up enough money. At that time, an advertisement appeared in the paper; a pony was selling for twenty-five dollars. I knew nothing about the pony except for a very generic description in the for sale ad. At that price, I was sure it was older than dirt, but all I cared about was that I had the money and a place to keep her. Hay cost fifty cents a bale at that time.

Around my tenth birthday, I *announced* to my parents—I didn't *ask*— that I was going to get a pony, and they could not stop me. I had the money, and I had a place to keep it. Problem solved. At that point, I think they realized I was not going to let this go, and they agreed to allow me to get the pony—but only if it didn't have three hooves in the grave. My first pony was a little brown and white pinto named Scout. We kept him at a boarding facility about twenty minutes from our home. Life was now perfect...

While growing up, I had several equine friends. First there was Scout and then Princess, a pretty bay Hackney pony. My first horse was Brandi. I bred Brandi twice, and she delivered a handsome chestnut colt named T-Bird; her second colt was a dark bay named Max.

In 1977, I went away to college at St. Mary's at Notre Dame, and my parents took care of Brandi at our home in Michigan. Eventually, however, she needed a new home. I was without a horse for the first time since I was ten years old.

Julie on Princess (top) and Brandi (bottom)

CHAPTER 3

Blind Dates Can Work

After college graduation, I moved to Orlando, Florida, working for the Upjohn Company as an agricultural sales representative. It was in Orlando that I met my husband, Bob. A friend and I were at a local nightclub, and she struck up a conversation with Bob's friend Rob. Rob kept insisting that I needed to meet his friend Bob. Rob said Bob was a great guy. Of course, I asked, "If he's so great, why is he still on the market?" Rob was insistent, so I gave him my number to pass on to Bob.

Bob called me one night, and we talked for forty-five minutes. I hung up the phone and thought *that was the most enjoyable and interesting conversation I've ever had with a total stranger.* We agreed to meet at a restaurant since I did not want him to know where I lived—in case he turned out to be a creeper. We were both twenty-seven at the time and had been on the dating scene long enough to know what we wanted in a future spouse; we were both tired of playing the dating game.

Our first date consisted of talking about all the forbidden topics: religion, politics, children, staying at home to raise the children, and careers. If we had been on the Dating Game TV show, we would have taken first place. All our answers matched, and two years later we were married.

When we first got married, we bought a house on two incomes since *our* plan was to wait a couple years before starting a family. However, God's plans were different.

Six months after we were married, I became pregnant with Allison. Andrew and Matt followed in the next two years. When Allison was born, I quit my job. We now had a house for which we had qualified while having two incomes. However, we now had another mouth to feed, diapers to buy, and half of the income. It was very stressful financially. However, Bob stayed strong with regards to our faith and priorities—to give to God out of the first fruits. With each paycheck, the first check he wrote was to the church as our tithe. I tried to convince him that God wouldn't mind if we scaled back a bit as we needed the money for bills and food and clothes. Bob was steadfast, however, saying that God would provide. *"Honor the Lord with your wealth, with the first fruits of all your produce; Then will your barns be filled with grain, with new wine your vats will overflow" (Prov. 3.9-10).*

Bob explained that tithing was not about the money; he was pretty sure they didn't use U.S. dollars or euros in Heaven or that God needed the money. Rather, that act of writing a check to the Church was affirming that we trusted God for *everything*. God also nudged us to take a course on Biblical financial principles. One of the fun facts we learned was that there are more scripture verses about money *than any other subject*—including love, salvation, sin, or forgiveness. God obviously knows our very human tendency to put more faith in the material, the visible, the tangible things of this world and therefore provided plenty of instruction in the Bible to help us avoid having other "gods." *"No one can serve two masters. Either you will hate the one and love the other, or you will be devoted to the one and despise the other. You cannot serve both God and money" (Matt. 6.24).*

Those years in Orlando were full of God's hand upon us as He taught us to fully rely on *Him*. Just when we thought we couldn't pay a bill or desperately needed new tires for the van, literally, we would get a check in the mail. One time I received a check for almost $400 that was a refunded deposit from an electric company back when I was single. And the bill for the tires for the van was $408. ***"Trust in the Lord with all your heart and lean not on your own understanding; in all your ways submit to Him, and he will make your paths straight" (Prov. 3.5).***

CHAPTER 4

Walking the Talk

In 1996, Bob asked his company for a transfer to Indianapolis, so we could be closer to family. His family was in Pennsylvania and my family was in Michigan. We hoped we could sell our home in Florida by ourselves to save commission fees.

We had a garage sale one weekend, and an attractive blonde woman walked up the driveway. We started talking, and I mentioned that we were having the garage sale since we were getting ready to list our home for the move to Indy. She told me that she knew a family who wanted to move to our neighborhood; I offered to show her the house so she could describe it to her friend. We had not listed it with a realtor yet and were still hoping to sell it by ourselves.

One week later, we had an offer on the house, and it was the attractive blonde lady—there was no "friend"—it had been her all along. They had a family of four young boys, and our house was perfect for them. **"Give thanks in all circumstances; for this is God's will for you in Christ Jesus"(1 Thes. 5.18).**

When we moved to Westfield, Indiana, in June 1996, we had three children, four, five, and six years old. Before we left Florida, I started looking for Catholic schools in Westfield. I was told about Our Lady of Mount Carmel and called. Unfortunately, there was a very long waiting list, but they suggested that I try the new mission parish, St. Maria Goretti.

I called and talked to the receptionist and asked about the process to enroll our kids in kindergarten and second grade. She said we had to be members of the parish first; the paperwork could be faxed, and thirty minutes later we were parishioners at Saint Maria Goretti in Westfield. Next, enrollment for the kids—only one spot left in second grade. I asked what was needed, and by the grace of God and fax machines, Allison was enrolled in second grade and Andrew in kindergarten.

At Mass in Monseigneur Duncan Hall, every six months we would hear a pulpit announcement for something called "Christ Renews His Parish." There was a men's weekend and a women's weekend. It was supposed to be a chance to make new friends and increase your faith life—a lovely women's weekend getaway from the responsibilities of home, kids, and cooking—a chance to be pampered and fed with no dishes to clean. I know that sounds wonderful to most, but I was not "most." I had absolutely no desire *whatsoever* to hang out with a bunch of strange women (or women who were strangers to me), sing Kumbaya, and have someone tell me how to have a better relationship with the Lord. Thanks, but no thanks. I was perfectly content with my mediocre, lukewarm faith life. We went to Mass on Sundays, and the kids were going to Catholic school. Surely that was enough. *"I know your deeds, that you are neither cold nor hot. I wish you were either one or the other! So, because you are lukewarm—neither hot nor cold—I am about to spit you out of my mouth" (Rev. 3.15-16).*

In the spring of 1998, after two years of successfully dodging the Christ Renews His Parish team members handing out flyers at the doors trying to sign you up after a pulpit announcement, for some reason after this particular pulpit announcement, my husband caught my eye. I shrugged.

We couldn't find an excuse—no vacation, no plans, no out-of-town—nothing. We reluctantly decided to get it over with, and then they couldn't pester us anymore.

As was the custom, the husband attended the weekend first. When Bob came home after the weekend, he was a basket case. He was a hodgepodge of emotions. He was even more loving—apologetic even—saying he wanted to be a better husband and father. I was *freaked out*! It had to be a cult! They'd done something to him! He drank the juice! I was ready to cancel my weekend since I didn't want them messing with *my* mind.

Well, I did attend the weekend—talk about a *game changer*—it was *nothing* like I expected. I laughed, I cried—a lot—and I surrendered to the greatest Love of all. Jesus Christ became the Lord of my life—my reason for being—my joy. *"I will give you a new heart and put a new spirit in you; I will remove from you your heart of stone and give you a heart of flesh" (Ezek. 36.26).*

That weekend changed my life; there was no looking back. Each Mass ends with either the words, "Go forth and glorify the Lord by your life," or sometimes, "Go forth to love and serve the Lord." For the first time in my life, I really heard those words.

Question: What was I doing with my life to glorify the Lord or to love the Lord by serving even the least of my brothers?

Answer: Nothing.

CHAPTER 5

The Prayers of a Child

Remember in Chapter Two, Foreshadowing, the ten-year old determined girl who managed to get her first pony? That was in 1969. Fast forward almost thirty years later to 1998.

Our daughter, Allison, was ten years old. It was a Monday night and time for prayers and bed. Allison asked me, "When can we buy Paloma?" Paloma was a very well-bred, expensive Arabian mare at a nearby breeding farm where Allison and I would occasionally hang out or help to get our "horse fix." I told her there was no way we could ever afford a horse like Paloma, and we especially could not afford the board bill—about the same as an expensive car payment. At that moment a stroke of genius hit me. I advised her, "Why don't you pray, and when God wants us to have a horse, He will provide one." She seemed to think that was reasonable and began to make the sign of the cross as I left the room.

I, on the other hand, felt very smug at my cleverness and glibly pointed my finger at the ceiling in the hallway, looked heavenward, and said, "It's *your* problem now." I had successfully handed that off to God and was probably now in the running for "Mom of the Year." When she didn't get a pony, she could take it up with *Him*. I am cringing as I write this.

The next morning, Tuesday, at 8:30, the phone rang. The caller was Mike, the man who owned the farm where Paloma was. He told me they were selling the farm and since I had helped them out, *they wanted to give Paloma to me—papers and all—for free!* At that moment, I looked over my shoulder. I think I expected to see God pointing His finger at me and saying, "It's *your* problem now, Julie." I guess two can play that game. **"Jesus answered him, 'It is also written; Do not put the LORD your God to the test'" (Matt. 4.7).**

La Paloma

Even though we had just been given a very nice, very expensive horse—the actual horse for which my daughter had prayed—we still could not afford to board her. I took a chance though and called my boss at Viking Meadows, a Standardbred breeding farm in Westfield where I worked part time, doing some computer work and helping on the farm with whatever they needed. (Again, I was getting my "horse fix.") I asked my boss, "If I should happen to find myself the new owner of a horse, could I trade my paycheck for a spot in the fields to keep her?" After about a millisecond of hesitation, he said, "Sure!"

So now, ten hours after I pointed my finger at God and challenged Him, not only did I have the *exact horse* for which my daughter had prayed but also a free place to keep her. And if that wasn't enough for me to recognize that I was starting a journey...

We told the kids we were now the proud owners of La Paloma. That day after school, Allison came running into the house, out of breath and barely able to speak. "Mom, Mom! Do you know what "La Paloma" means in Spanish?" I had no idea. She said, "It means 'dove' and also 'Holy Spirit!'"—which, of course, I immediately verified on the internet. *"As soon as Jesus was baptized, he went up out of the water. At that moment heaven was opened, and he saw the Spirit of God descending like a dove and alighting on him" (Matt. 3.16).*

A breadcrumb—now what?

CHAPTER 6

A Place That Does "Something with Kids and Horses"

Not long after we were gifted with La Paloma, a friend at St. Maria Goretti told me there was "this place in Carmel that does something with kids and horses," and that I should go check it out. Yeah right, on the eighth day of the week.

Well, lo and behold, I just *happened* to find myself on Towne Road not long after—an area of town I rarely *ever* went to—and I spotted a very small sign on the side of the road. This was the place my friend mentioned that did "something with kids and horses," and somehow the car turned into the driveway. I pulled up in front of a very large barn and decided to go in and see what this place was all about.

I walked into an observation room that looked out onto a large indoor riding arena. In that arena was an enormous Clydesdale-cross horse upon which sat a tiny boy with Down syndrome. That little man bossed that big horse all over the arena. "Turn here!" "Go there!" "Stop!" The entire time, he had a huge grin on his face and was *master* of his universe in that moment. Watching her son, his mother stood next to me at the window with tears of joy, hope, and awe as she saw him pilot that horse around the arena. Now, I was in tears. I knew I had to take part in this. That day, I signed up to volunteer.

For the next two years, I volunteered at this facility and another center where the physical therapists, occupational therapists, and speech/language pathologists used horses as a treatment tool of therapy to help children with special needs learn to speak, gain more function and control over their bodies, and become more independent with activities of daily living. I learned how the movement of the horse impacted not only the physical abilities of the riders but also their emotional, psychological, and spiritual lives.

About this time, my boss at Viking Meadows asked if I wanted Viking Sunrise, also known as "Beamer." Beamer is a beautiful, dark bay Standardbred Pacer gelding—and very tall. He is a true gentle giant. After having a slight injury on the racetrack, he was unable to continue his racing career. Beamer had been retired to Viking Meadows and was a barn favorite because of his sweet personality. He lived in the same pasture as La Paloma. I trained him to accept a saddle and rider, and now Allison and I had two horses to ride.

Viking Sunrise aka Beamer

La Paloma means "dove" or "Holy Spirit." Viking Sunrise symbolizes "light," "Sunrise on Easter morning,"—the "Risen Christ." Another breadcrumb…

CHAPTER 7

What We See; What We Don't See

Reaching into the Rain Forest

What we see: This rider is reaching into the rain forest to pinch a green rain drop or grasp two blue rain drops. She is also looking for a tiny grasshopper clinging to a dusky, green leaf. How many pretty butterflies can she count?

What we don't see: What is happening in the rider's body beneath the fun and excitement of discovering the rain forest while riding a horse? Little fingers and hands are practicing pinching and grasping. Neck muscles are working hard to support the head so the eyes can visually track, team, and coordinate with the hands in order to touch or grab the swaying raindrops. Core muscles are engaged to stabilize the spine and pelvis in the sitting position so she can reach up and out.

Riding through the Carwash

What we see: This child is riding through the horse carwash as strips of flannel flow gently over his face. Watch as his arms reach up to try and catch the wiggling strips in the breeze. He can also play hide and seek, peek-a-boo, or open and close the curtain as he rides his pretty pony through this sensory station.

What we don't see: What is happening in the rider's body beneath the fun and excitement of discovering the horse "carwash" while learning to ride a horse? As the rider is distracted by other sights, sounds, colors, and rhythmic sensation of riding the horse, the soft flow of the flannel over his face and head is desensitizing his facial skin so he can learn to tolerate having his face touched and his hair washed. Each time he rides through the horse carwash he becomes less reactive to light touch.

Visually tracking Elmo

What we see: A rider is coming around the corner in the arena and we shout, "Look! There is bright red Elmo. Can you see him? Let's go grab him!"

What we don't see: What is happening in the rider's body beneath the fun and excitement of looking for Elmo while riding a horse? As she visually tracks Elmo while moving through space, she works hard to keep her eyes focused and working together. Carefully she then raises her arm and hand to coordinate with her eyes and brain in order to reach out and touch Elmo as she rides underneath the Flying Circus mobile.

Nellie Hugs

What we see: This young man is getting a warm, gigantic, backwards hug from Nellie as she walks rhythmically around the arena.

What we don't see: What is happening in the rider's body beneath the fuzzy cuddles? He is receiving warm, rhythmic, bilateral, sensory information to his entire body as Nellie walks around the arena. This brisk, symmetrical movement is purposeful. The processing of this information in the brain helps increase our rider's neuromuscular organization and ability to regulate his thoughts and behaviors. This therapy activity is very helpful to riders who have stress and anxiety. With the body's sensory systems organized, the child is in optimal learning-ready mode.

CHAPTER 8

PATH Intl. Training

Two years into volunteering as a side walker and barn buddy for hippotherapy centers, I discovered therapeutic riding. Becoming a therapeutic riding instructor was something *I could do*. I was not a physical therapist (PT), occupational therapist (OT) or speech-language pathologist (SLP), but I could be trained and certified to teach people with disabilities how to ride a horse!

The governing body of therapeutic riding and equine assisted activities and therapy (EAAT) is now called Professional Association of Therapeutic Horsemanship (PATH, Intl.). It was formerly called North American Riding for the Handicapped Association (NARHA). The certification program took about two years for me to complete, and I became certified in 2004.

Continuing education is mandatory in order to retain certification. Every year, I attend various conferences, seminars, and workshops to stay on top of the ever-changing world of equine-assisted activities. As more and more professions discover the wide range of benefits experienced on or around horses, the greater the need for standards and professional guidelines.

The earliest recognition of the horse's ability to help heal was discovered during times of war. The sooner wounded soldiers were reunited with their horses, the faster they healed. Now, modern-day use of horses to heal includes hippotherapy, therapeutic riding, family counseling, youth and teen mental health assistance, equine-facilitated psychotherapy, and equine-assisted learning. Horses for Heroes veteran programs and even corporate team-building workshops use horses as part of the therapy team.

CHAPTER 9

Levi's Story

Levi was a three-year-old, adorable powerhouse with Down Syndrome. He had a bright and sunny disposition and just knew everyone wanted to be his friend. What he didn't know, however, was how to walk.

At three years old, he was very strong and healthy. All his muscles, tendons, ligaments, bones, and joints were in the right places and in working order, so technically, he should have been able to walk. However, for some reason, he would not, could not. His parents had tried all sorts of therapies and techniques, to no avail. Finally, in desperation and out of options, a therapist told them to try "horse therapy." She was at a loss of what to do but had heard positive things about using horses as part of a therapeutic program.

Levi came out to Reins of Grace and immediately fell in love with Dundee. He had no hesitation or fear when he sat on her for the first time. He was eager to learn and was engaged and focused as I started to teach him how to tell his horse to walk on by tapping her neck. For his first lesson, Levi sat on Dundee as she walked around the arena for about twenty minutes. When I took him off Dundee at the end of the lesson, his legs began bicycling in the air, or "air walking."

The walking motion of the horse very closely mimics the walking motion of a human. We know that the three-dimensional movement of the horse is the sensory information that traveled through Levi's legs, hips, trunk, neck, and head, along the neural pathways to the brain for processing. In this case, the brain took the information and created a map—a road map of when and how the muscles should move for walking.

After just four sessions on Dundee, Levi began taking his first steps with assistance from his parents. The walking movement of the horse was the sensory information the brain needed to tell Levi's body how to walk.

CHAPTER 10

The "Ah-ha" Moment

At one of the other centers, I met a single mother who was working two jobs so her son could ride just twice a month.

Hippotherapy (using a horse as part of a treatment protocol by physical therapists, occupational therapists, and speech/language pathologists) is a very expensive treatment since a licensed professional is involved as well as the expense of a horse. The money needed for the care of horses includes buying acreage, buildings, fencing, feed, veterinary care, equipment, insurance, and labor, just to name a few. Insurance rarely pays for therapy, and if they do, not very many treatment sessions are covered.

I could only imagine the frustration of a parent whose child has special needs, discovering an extremely beneficial treatment that the child *loves,* and then being told, "You can't have that therapy because you don't have the money."

Paloma Kisses

I knew then why I had been given La Paloma and Beamer. My mission became paying the gift of the horses forward and offering therapeutic riding lessons free of charge.

La Paloma and Beamer were still being boarded at Viking Meadow. I continued to work there part time and started giving a couple lessons per week. I did not advertise; word of mouth brought riders to me. When people asked how much lessons cost, I told them, "It is a God-thing, and I am paying it forward, so there is no charge." Unfortunately, the adage, "you get what you pay for," seemed to apply here. People took advantage of getting this free service and were not as committed to keeping their appointments. Finally, I asked families to pay the horses, since they were doing all the work. The forms of payment were apples, carrots, or fly spray. This seemed to rectify the situation; parents had some "skin in the game" and felt there was more value in the lesson if they had to pay for it.

Eventually, people brought loaded grocery sacks of apples and carrots! It got to the point where the "beer fridge" no longer had any beer in it due to the pounds and pounds of apples and carrots. Bob put his foot down and said, "If they are spending that much on apples and carrots, maybe a $20 bill would be better—and we would get the beer fridge back."

CHAPTER 11

"You Have to Move the Horses"

"You have to move the horses. The farm is being sold to developers." Those words were like a death sentence to me. I was still newly certified and only starting to teach when my boss told me I had to find a new place for La Paloma and Beamer. Nothing had changed about our financial situation in terms of boarding *two* horses.

Our only options were to sell the horses, board them, and give lessons at a boarding facility (too expensive and too difficult to control safety of the riders in a public facility), or move to the country and set up shop on our own property.

"No. We can't afford it." "No. I don't like horses." "No. I don't like the smell of manure." "No. I really hate flies." "No. I don't like mowing." "No. I don't like living in the sticks." "No. It's too much work." "Did I say NO yet?" So *obviously*, such strong feelings from my husband, indicated he did *not* think that what *I* felt was a calling from God, nor did he feel God was calling *him* to this ministry.

Well, of course I must have read the "signs" wrong. This must have been, "Julie wants horses in the back yard but will disguise it as a riding ministry." The doubts set in. If Bob and I were at such opposite ends of the spectrum, surely God wouldn't ask that of him—which meant us? If everything about this potential ministry was so far out of Bob's wheelhouse, could it truly be a calling from God? Would God really put him, me, and our marriage to such a test?

Yes, Yes, and Yes. *"Therefore, I urge you, brothers and sisters, in view of God's mercy, to offer your bodies as a living sacrifice, holy and pleasing to God—this is your true and proper worship. ² Do not conform to the pattern of this world, but be transformed by the renewing of your mind. Then you will be able to test and approve what God's will is—his good, pleasing and perfect will"* (Rom. 12.1-5).

I couldn't help myself; I kept looking for properties and I would often find myself on the backroads in Westfield, Sheridan, Carmel, and Noblesville, searching. Somehow, I felt I was going to drive by "the spot" and would know in my heart that God had chosen it. More often than not, I found myself looking at "For Sale" signs in front of an 1800's dilapidated farmhouse—probably with no running water or electricity and so overgrown you couldn't even see if there was a driveway—but ever hopeful that maybe this was our fixer-upper. After all, didn't following God always require a little sacrifice?

Many times, when we would fight about looking for land, selling our current home, and building "out in the sticks," I would allow the doubts to win and I would quit. I would quit looking for land, quit listening to God, quit thinking about the many, many children in Hamilton county alone who desperately needed this type of riding therapy but couldn't afford it. I would quit thinking about the single mom with two jobs and the fact that insurance *might* only cover a small portion of the fees. I would quit thinking about minimal insurance coverage that gave families a taste of how beneficial riding could be for their child and then cruelly take it away from them.

Bob would go to the Adoration Chapel at our church every Saturday morning and would pray about the decision of whether we should buy land and start a therapeutic riding ministry. When he got home, I'd run eagerly to him with my hands clasped hopefully and ask, "Well, what did He say? *What did He say?*" And he would gruffy answer, "He didn't say 'Yes'—but He didn't say 'No.'" What kind of answer was *that*?

I, on the other hand, still felt this was a calling or vocation directly from God. After all, look at how God gave us Paloma and Beamer (Spirit and Light) and how I stumbled across the therapy riding center and subsequently became a certified therapeutic riding instructor, already building a clientele.

Now we were being asked to *really* stretch—to *really* trust God. On paper, Bob was right. We couldn't afford our own place. Also, we were completely at odds with one another. Bob refused to even entertain the possibility that in the right circumstances we could make it work—and I couldn't let it go.

It was during this impasse that my parents sold the family home in Michigan and gifted my brothers, sisters, and me with some money from the sale of the house and land. This opened the (barn) door for land. Another breadcrumb?

After crunching the numbers for the thousandth time, Bob finally gave me permission to look for land, but he had a couple of restrictions: no more than five acres, and it had to be no more than five miles from St. Maria Goretti. *If* we could find such a property, we would just "sit on it" to make sure we could afford it and then slowly work towards building a house and fencing for the horses.

I was ecstatic. I could hardly wait to scour the surrounding countryside for our new farm. Bob, on the other hand, was secretly gleeful. He felt very confident that there could not be any five-acre property within a five-mile radius of St. Maria Goretti that we could afford. Meanwhile, that got me off his back, and we both were happy.

In early Spring of 2006, I found a five-acre bean field on 206th Street in Sheridan that we could afford. *It was exactly 4.9 miles from the house to the main door of St. Maria Goretti Catholic Church.*

Another breadcrumb…

CHAPTER 12

For Sale by Owner—Again

We had land! The next big hurdle: selling a house and building one at the same time. Bob was dragging his feet a bit since he knew the market and knew we would never be able to afford to list the house, pay commissions, and still have enough to start a new build. Since we had sold our home in Florida in essentially one day at a garage sale, I suggested we try "For Sale by Owner."

I filled out all the necessary paperwork and put a FSBO sign in the yard. We had one showing. Finally, an agent contacted us and said she had a client who wanted to see both our house and another available house in our neighborhood. We arranged for the agent to come to our house one Saturday morning so I could show her around and point out some upgraded features and benefits of our home. The plan for that morning was for Bob to take the kids out to breakfast, and then I would leave before the clients arrived.

The agent and I were in the basement, and I was pointing out some finishes we had done when we heard a big commotion upstairs. My first thought was that Bob had brought the kids back early for some reason—and the timing couldn't be worse since the prospective buyer was due any minute, and I had to get out of there. The realtor and I raced upstairs to the front door and saw a family of strangers standing in our foyer. Having misunderstood the agent, they thought they were supposed to be at our house first, at 9:00.

As I was trying to quietly back out, the woman saw a crucifix on the wall in the foyer and asked if we were Catholic and did we belong to Our Lady of Mt. Carmel Church? I replied we were indeed Catholic, and Our Lady of Mt. Carmel held a very special place in my heart because I had gone through the Christ Renews His Parish (CRHP) program at OLMC; however, we were members of St. Maria Goretti.

At that point, she burst into tears and said she had just gone through the CRHP program the weekend before, and it had changed her life. Next thing I knew, we were hugging, crying, and talking like old friends—filled with the joy and wonder of our new life in Christ.

We continued to talk about CRHP; when I told her the year I had made the weekend (*fifteen years earlier*), she got a funny look on her face and asked if I knew her sister. Talk about a small world. One of my teammates on the weekend was this woman's sister!

Are you starting to see a pattern? Yes, they bought the house.

CHAPTER 13

Green Acres Is the Place for Me

After we found a builder for the house, we broke ground for the basement in November of 2006; we moved to the farm in August of 2007. We had been able to fence in one field and move the horses to their new home; however, we had no barns for shelter, feed, or storage. Previously, this had been a five-acre bean field, so we were starting from scratch.

Shortly after we moved to the farm, one of my rider's parents contacted me and asked if I needed materials for a barn. The husband had taken apart a couple of old barns and had beams and siding he offered to give us. Amazingly, we had enough materials to make a 10' x 24' three-sided run-in shed. The horses were going to have a 10' x 14' space for shelter, and I would have a 10' by 10' space for hay and equipment storage. We had only one small problem: Bob and I had *never* built anything. We didn't even own power tools. However, would God have called us out here and then abandoned us? *"...for He has said, 'I will never forsake you or abandon you. Thus, we may say with confidence, 'The Lord is my helper, I will not be afraid'"* **(Heb. 13.5-6).**

Earlier in the Spring, we had ventured out to look at our half-built house and met our new neighbors, Dan, Kandi, and their son, Brent. At the time, they were finishing building their own house right next door.

It just so happened that we had an immediate connection since they were dedicated Christians with a deep love for Jesus. The fact that our riding ministry was Christ-inspired and Christ-centered was a perfect fit for us all.

It just so happened that Kandi had grown up on a farm in Canada and had experience with all sorts of animals, including horses. When I told her what we were going to be doing on the farm, she instantly volunteered to help. She was my first side-walker for the therapy ministry. We had not even moved the horses to the farm yet, so I picked Kandi up on lesson days and we drove to Viking Meadows to do lessons.

It just so happened that when Dan saw the load of materials sitting in the driveway, he asked what we were going to do with it. We told him it was donated material for a run-in shed but that Bob and I had *no idea* where to even begin. We had never even set a post.

*It just so happene*d that Dan and his son, Brent, were quite skilled and knowledgeable about building since they had done quite a bit of the actual building of their house.

It just so happened that Dan asked if we would like them to lend a hand. Imagine us turning *that* down.

Dan and Brent engineered the entire project, and Bob and I had our first experience with hands-on learning: setting posts, using table saws, working with circular saws, joists, and joist hangers. We became familiar with the myriad of fasteners, screws, nails and bolts—and how important *level* was.

We were in business! To this day, the barn is still being used, and we have expanded it with four different projects. Serving as stable and storage, it was our "corporate headquarters" for the first seven years.

Corporate Headquarters

CHAPTER 14

Becky's Story

Let's set the scene: a teenage girl with a very dysfunctional homelife. She didn't know how to trust or communicate effectively with peers or adults. Due to this unstable, "survival-of-the-fittest" background, she had developed anxiety as well as defensive and protective mechanisms such as bullying, aggression, and dominance. Her only concern was how she could benefit from any social interaction. Essentially, she had no real friendships. Her self-esteem was low; she didn't feel like she had a purpose or that she was wanted or needed.

How could a herd of horses help Becky? What could they show her or teach her? How could that translate to human relationships in other areas of her life, including school and work?

On Becky's first day at Reins of Grace, we started with herd observation. Five horses were loose in the arena. I instructed Becky to watch the horses and their interactions with each other. With keen perception, Becky was observing Dundee looking at Sadie, putting her ears back against her head, and switching her tail. Sadie gave a half-hearted swish of her tail in

Dundee's general direction but then proceeded to go to the other side of the arena. Becky said she felt Dundee was bossing Sadie.

Next, Becky watched Pearlie and Nellie, a mother and daughter, stick together and generally avoid Dundee. The horses did some back and forth smack talk—pinning ears back, lowering their necks, stretching and shaking their heads, and curling their nostrils—but they all kept a respectful distance from each other. This behavior reminded Becky of rival gangs in school—a lot of posturing and posing.

Beamer, the lone male in the group and the largest of the horses, was able to walk anywhere he wanted, and all the horses gave way and did not challenge him. He could eat hay first, and none of the other horses tried to run him off. Becky concluded that he was definitely "top dog" of the herd.

Without realizing it, Becky was learning to identify social cues the horses were using amongst themselves to communicate and establish boundaries. Each horse had recognized its role and importance within the herd, based on its unique characteristics and abilities. These roles would ultimately contribute to the overall well-being, stability, and safety of the herd when cooperation and protection became necessary. When the chips were down, they did not compete, they collaborated. This is what Becky was seeking, but she didn't know how to effectively communicate and integrate with a "herd" of her peers at school. Understanding language and social nuance is critical for survival and stability in any herd or group—whether horses or humans.

One of Becky's struggles at school was not taking the time to observe and understand the social cues of her peers. Because of her protective mechanisms, she automatically went on the defensive and didn't allow for the give and take of two-way conversation; it was her way or the highway. She rarely got the desired response or positive feedback from those interactions. This lack of relationship and acceptance left her frustrated and angry and became a vicious cycle.

Because communication with the horses was without language, Becky couldn't use her habitual tricks of dominating the conversation, bullying, or intimidating. She had to learn how to communicate with the horses using a language *they* could understand. Becky had to be open to new ways to communicate if she wanted to be able to work with the horses. Most importantly, she had to see and understand the situation *from the horse's point of view.*

In our next session, I had Becky go into the arena and "pick a horse" to be her partner. Having to make the initial social overture, Becky could not rely on her old habits of verbal domination and aggression. The horses watched her walk across the arena, but as she strode purposefully toward them, they avoided her outstretched hand. Beamer even snorted and trotted away. They turned their collective rumps toward her and stayed out of reach.

Becky's first reaction was anger. She was being rejected—again. I asked her if she understood their behavior and if she had any thoughts as to why they turned away from her. After a few minutes of shuffling her feet and looking at the dirt, she quietly asked, "Are they afraid of me? Or maybe I was moving too fast?"

I asked her to figure out how she could be more inviting and less demanding—less threatening to the herd. Becky asked if she could just wait in the arena and see if they would come to her. I told her to try it and observe the horses' reactions.

As she stood quietly in a neutral position, vulnerable and open, sweet Sadie Sue, the matriarch of the herd, came to her and sniffed her outstretched hand. Sadie licked her lips, took a deep breath, and stood quietly with Becky. Slowly, one by one, each horse came to Becky and offered a neck to be patted or a shoulder to be scratched. Becky was accepted into the herd.

That day, Becky learned how to look at the herd (and eventually her peer group) as a cohesive cooperative designed to support and protect each member of the group, not something to be infiltrated and dominated.

She had to learn what *they* were thinking, what *they* wanted and needed in order to respond to *their* needs. She could not waltz in, intruding and imposing her wants and needs on the herd (or peer group).

Working with the horses taught Becky how to see communication and relationships as a "give-and-take" process and how to accept responsibility for her own actions and decisions in this dynamic. As she progressed in her understanding of "horse language," this helped her transition to more productive and positive social interactions with her peers and teachers.

This is how a herd of horses helped Becky.

CHAPTER 15

Reins of Grace Therapeutic Riding Center

We started off as the Beamer-Paloma Center, and we were a limited liability corporation (LLC). We had two horses and served approximately six riders a week from May thru October. Funding the ministry out of our own pockets, Bob and I paid for feed, specialty/adaptive riding equipment, veterinary care, hoof care, fencing for the pastures and paddocks, and additions to our original 10' x 24' building. Additionally, we fed and cared for goats and chickens that we had added for our sensory integration program and petting zoo component. Our Mission Statement was to "provide therapeutic riding services to those in need, regardless of ability to pay," so there was very little income from the lessons themselves to help defray the endless expenses. However, the bottom line of our ministry was to "pay it forward," and if God had brought us this far...

However, I was more the visionary (not bothered by silly details like money) and Bob was the realist. Simply put, *everything* was very costly, and when we wrote everything out on paper, *it couldn't be done.* Numbers don't lie, and they just didn't add up; we could not afford to run the farm and ministry. This was a great challenge for both of us, but Bob especially as the sole provider for the family.

"Trust in the LORD with all your heart and lean not on your own understanding; in all your ways acknowledge him, and he will make your paths straight" (Prov. 3.5-6).

In the meantime, somehow the ministry was growing, and we were getting more requests for lessons. We purchased a third horse named Dundee from a horse rescue facility. In January of 2010, I had right shoulder surgery and knew I was going to need a much shorter horse to allow for continued rehab of that shoulder. We found a little brown pony named Sadie on Craigslist and she was the perfect size.

By now we had expanded the original 10' x 24' barn by adding a porch roof. Several times a year the weather would blow in from the east and flood the barn, making the mud floor a soupy mess. The porch roof was our second addition and blocked much of the weather. Perhaps it doesn't sound like much, but when you're cleaning up after four horses seven days a week, it makes it much easier and provides much better shelter for the horses.

Soupy Mess

After we built the porch roof, we converted the hay and storage area to a stall and added another 10' x 24' section on the west side of the original barn. That new space became a storage space for equipment, feed, and riding gear. It also became the place where the families would go to get their child's helmet on to prepare for the lesson. Yes, it was organized right up to the rafters, since it served multiple purposes.

Next, we added another 10' x 24' bay to the west of that for more storage of equipment and the tractor. At this point we were up to four horses and seeing twelve riders a week. We had also expanded the arena two more times.

About this time, around 2010, I had a conversation with my friend Mike in the Adoration Chapel at Saint Maria Goretti. I would go to Adoration at 8 o'clock on Wednesday mornings, and Mike would come in at 9 o'clock. He's a big Notre Dame football fan, and we would exchange football news as we changed shifts.

One morning he pulled me aside and told me I needed to meet Al and Sheri Peterson. He had known them since high school, and they were some of the best people on the planet. He said that Sheri was a speech therapist and wanted to incorporate equine therapy into her private practice; however, she was not a "horse person" and was looking for someone to help with that aspect of her practice. Knowing that I had started the therapeutic riding ministry, Mike thought we could help each other.

He gave me her number, and I called her. I think we talked on the phone for about forty-five minutes; I felt like I was talking to a long-lost sister. When we met to exchange ideas about how we could work together, we couldn't talk fast enough. Sheri became a volunteer that year and has continued to volunteer at least twice a week, never charging for her speech therapy services. *"And God is able to make all grace abound to you, so that having all sufficiency in all things at all times, you may abound in every good work" (2 Cor. 9.8).*

We have always closed in the winter since it is too cold for our small riders to tolerate lessons in the cold outdoor weather, and we had no indoor arena at the time. After Sheri's first year as a volunteer, she approached me before lessons began in the spring of 2013 and announced, "Over the winter Al and I were talking. We decided that you need a fundraiser—and we're going to host it for you."

Al and Sheri's property is among one of the most picturesque farms in Hamilton County. The house, surrounded by giant evergreens, had been built in 1906 and sits on top of a hill with a gorgeous old hand-hewn barn, built in 1860, overlooking the west pastures. When they bought their property in Cicero, they felt a strong calling from God to use the property for His will in whatever capacity that might be. After prayer and discernment that winter, they decided that God was calling them to help Reins of Grace Therapeutic Riding Center get on its feet. The first Peterson Farmfest Hog Roast was held in 2013 at Al and Sheri's farm in Cicero.

It was a simple concept; have a hog roast, great blue grass music, a gorgeous outdoor venue, games and activities for the kids, and at the same time raise some money to help fund the programs and offset operating expenses at Reins of Grace. The very first hog roast was quite memorable. Of course, since the event was being held outside, the weather was a concern. We all watched The Weather Channel obsessively—as if by sheer will, we could guarantee no rain. On the day of the hog roast, there was a 40% chance of rain. I remember my mom calling and asking if we were going to cancel because of the prediction. I could see dark purple clouds surrounding Al and Sheri's farm. It was around 4:00 pm, when the gates were to open, and we were bracing for the storm. There was nothing we could do. The stage was set for the bands, the hog had been roasting since Friday, and tents were set up for food and drinks. There was no turning back. Suddenly, a straight-line wind blew across the top of the hill where we were set up. One single tent crumpled like a piece of paper—then nothing. No more wind and even a peek of sunshine. It was *pouring* in Westfield, just a few miles away. In every direction we looked, there were angry, purple clouds surrounding us on the top of the hill. Not one drop of rain fell on Al and Sheri's farm. An invisible glass dome protected us. The first Farmfest Hog Roast was a huge, rain-free success! ***"But let all who take refuge in you be glad; let them ever sing for joy. Spread your protection over them, that those who love your name may rejoice in you" (Psalm. 5.11).***

I would be remiss if I did not take this opportunity to express my infinite gratitude to the *multitudes* of individuals, church groups, families, businesses, musicians—and especially Al and Sheri Peterson—who not only made the Farmfest fundraisers possible, but also *perfect* successes. I use the word *perfect* because through these Hands and Feet of Christ, God provided *exactly everything* we needed—from donated foods, helpers, and services to the gifts and donations from the yearly fundraisers that sustained our ministry *for six years*. ***"…Our Father, who art in Heaven… give us this day our daily bread" (Luke 11.2-3).***

Peterson Farmfest Fundraiser

Many people had asked and were willing to donate money and equipment to Beamer-Paloma Center, but since we started out in 2007 as an LLC, we could not issue a tax-exempt receipt. When we had initially consulted a lawyer about becoming a not-for-profit, it would have cost approximately $10,000-$15,000 for an attorney to do the paperwork. That was not an option for us. Additionally, we had also been told that it was very difficult to be granted not-for-profit status.

In February of 2012, I made a trip to Florida to visit my parents. I had lunch with my dad, and he asked again about the possibility of filing the paperwork to become a not-for-profit. He asked if I knew any attorneys. I didn't think I knew any attorneys; however, at that moment a name popped into my head. One of my sisters from Christ Renews was an attorney. As I remembered her, I understood the Holy Spirit was prompting me to take the next step and call her. *"Likewise the Spirit helps us in our weakness. For we do not know what to pray for as we ought, but the Spirit himself intercedes for us with groanings too deep for words"* *(Rom. 8.26).*

When I got home from the trip, I called my teammate and asked for her help. She did not practice that type of law; however, she gave me the name of someone whom she felt would be able to help us. I contacted him, and he agreed to meet. He was a dedicated Christian and offered without hesitation to guide us through the tax-exempt filing process, pro bono. After beginning the paperwork, I met with him several times for clarification and guidance. In 2013, we were granted tax-exempt status as a not-for-profit organization—Reins of Grace Therapeutic Riding Center.

I couldn't have navigated the murky waters of government bureaucracy without him. This was yet another connection through the Christ Renews His Parish program and a reminder that God was directing all of this—I just simply needed to trust Him. *"Seek the Kingdom of God above all else, and he will give you everything you need"* *(Luke 12.31).*

In the springtime, many days would be rainy, windy, and sloppy, causing unsafe footing, so lessons had to be canceled. In the summertime, there were weeks when the temperature and heat index were close to 100, which not only took the fun out of the lessons but posed a danger to some of our riders who had trouble regulating their body temperatures. In the fall, we would once again end up with rainy conditions, which would affect the footing and therefore the safety of our sidewalkers, horses, and riders. A cold snap could make a child shiver so hard and contract muscles so intensely that the beneficial, three-dimensional movement of the horse could not be absorbed.

It was frustrating and sad for many of the parents to tell their three-year-old or four-year-old child at the last minute, "You can't ride the horse today because of the weather." At that age, children don't understand. All they know is they don't get to see their horse that day. Additionally, the beneficial outcome provided by the consistency of the therapeutic riding was adversely affected. It only took one season of these weather-related cancellations before we started praying for an indoor arena.

We lost so many lessons because of weather that it became critical for the future of our ministry to be able to offer our services consistently to our little riders. We had fundraisers, corporate sponsors, and individual families who were overwhelmingly generous, and along with cashing in a significant portion of our retirement, in November of 2014 the 70' x 150' indoor arena and stable area were completed.

Before the Arena

Building the Arena

Reins of Grace Indoor Riding Arena

With the indoor facility, we were able to add an additional four weeks of therapy services for the children. I remember the *very first day* of lessons in the spring of 2015; it rained cats and dogs. Standing under the cover and safety of the new roof, Sheri and I looked out at the spring deluge. We gave thanks to God for this beautiful barn, beautiful spring rain, and the fact that we didn't have to cancel the very first day of spring lessons. We thought this was God's rather humorous and ironic way of letting us know that we were on the right track and following His will.

CHAPTER 16

Raising Snakes

After building the indoor arena, we grew exponentially in terms of the number of riders served and the variety of programs and services we offered. However, as the property continued to be developed, it also needed to be maintained. Mowing was an overwhelming, unending, brutal, bouncy, back-breaking chore. Weed whacking the fence line was worse—bugs, poison ivy, spider webs, and sweat. Three hundred fifty-six fence posts constantly needed to be painted. Goat fencing and chicken wire continually needed to be mended. Stalls needed to be cleaned, water tanks power washed—repeat, repeat, repeat. And, to top it all off, for some reason we were *not* getting any younger, more flexible, or stronger.

Ironically, as a confirmation from God that we were in fact doing His will, He provided financial resources, volunteers, helpers, equipment—*everything we needed*—this caused the Enemy to sit up and take notice, and make no mistake, there is a constant spiritual battle for our souls. The financial sacrifices that had to be made every day were painfully apparent; often, doubts were raised, and God's will was questioned. ***"For we do not wrestle against flesh and blood, but against the rulers, against***

the authorities, against the cosmic powers over this present darkness, against the spiritual forces of evil in the heavenly places" (Eph. 6.12).

Due to the stress of constant, back-breaking labor and financial sacrifice, Bob became vulnerable to spiritual attack and would slip into a dark place full of resentment and anger. During those times, he would tell me how much he hated pretty much everything about his role in this ministry. I, on the other hand, being raised with a "when the going gets tough, the tough get going" attitude, didn't understand why he complained so much. After all, he shouldn't grumble or blame me—this was God's work, and we were simply the caretakers of this ministry.

However, it distressed me to no end that he was so unhappy, continually asking when we could sell the farm and retire back to suburban life. Guilt set in, since I felt I was the cause of his unhappiness. I didn't know what to do; part of me had no sympathy since I thought he just wasn't being tough enough. Surely, I wouldn't be complaining if the shoe was on the other foot—or would I?

Raising snakes. What if Bob had come to me years ago and announced that God told him in *no uncertain terms* that He wanted Bob to raise snakes—that Bob knew in his very soul that God was calling him to this vocation, and as his wife, I was coming along for the ride. I had to participate. After all, it was a calling from God.

What if I had to build cages, fill water bowls, clean cages—which would mean I would have to actually *touch* a snake to move it from its cage—shop for rats to feed the snakes, and of course, adjust heat lamps so the little reptiles didn't catch a chill. There is *nothing*—and I do mean *nothing*—that I like, feel comfortable with, or could even get used to if it had *anything* to do with snakes.

I think God put that little scenario in my heart (and in my nightmares) to help me see Bob's perspective and to have a better understanding and empathy for what he had done and *continues to do*. This ministry was what I believed God had given me *in no uncertain terms*. If the shoe were indeed on the other foot—if Bob had been called to raise snakes—I don't think that I would have been strong enough or would have had unshakable faith and trust in his calling. Bob gave up *everything*—every comfort zone he has—and surrendered completely to my calling from God to this ministry. Not only did he accept the responsibility of running the farm but also trusted that God would make it work financially.

One morning, while in prayer, Bob asked God for the grace to be willing to give his life for Him if asked to do so. He heard back in his heart, "How can you ask this of me, when you can't serve me now without complaining." This made a profound impact on his attitude and his willingness to surrender completely to God's will.

Even though Bob humbly submitted to *God's will*, and we were finally on the same page, it does not mean that going forward will be easy for us. We will not be immune to suffering, challenges, and doubt. It will take constant vigilance for both of us to seek God's will in every circumstance. Continuously we must strive to honor one another and make sure we appreciate and acknowledge each other's sacrifice. ***"Listen to my voice and do all that I command you. Then you shall be my people, and I will be your God. Thus, I will fulfill the oath which I swore to your fathers, <u>to give them a land flowing with milk and honey; the one you have today</u>. Amen, Lord, I answered"*** *(Jer. 11.4-5).*

CHAPTER 17

Sensory Garden - To Bloom and Grow

In 2014, I met Nancy Hittle at the second annual Hog Roast fundraiser. Sheri had been eager for us to meet as she knew Nancy had such a heart for our special kids and a brilliant talent and passion for "all things that grow." I had mentioned to Sheri that I wanted to develop a "garden area" as a place for parents and siblings to explore, relax, or just enjoy the country. Someplace where they could take a deep breath and be still for a moment, taking time out from the crazy, hectic, stressful life of raising children and especially a child with special needs.

I met with Nancy and she not only became a volunteer to help sidewalk with the riders, but we also talked a little bit about a potential garden space. Explaining that I wanted a "little slice of Heaven," I told her that it would be a sensory experience for the whole family and especially the riders. Those were the only guidelines I gave Nancy. All my continuing education and research kept pointing to the benefit of physically moving through space while experiencing sensory input. This combination of movement and sensory experience facilitates learning, increases and improves physical and psychological function, which leads to greater independence.

We had a 50' x 60' foot chicken and goat yard in front of the big barn that could be used for a sensory garden. She said she would come up with something.

Goat and chicken yard before the Sensory Garden

Next thing I knew, an exquisite, detailed artist rendering had been created, detailing a space that could *only* be called a piece of heaven on earth.

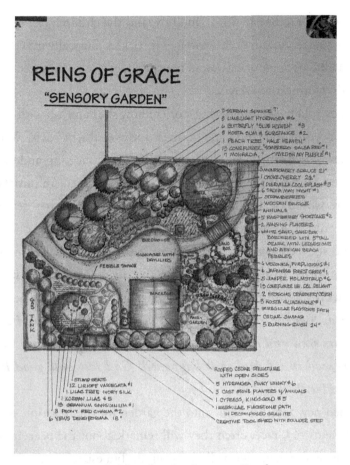

Nancy's Plan for the Sensory Garden

Everything in the garden was chosen for its multiple sensory characteristics. A self-pollinating peach tree grows where the children can sit in the shade and pick peaches to eat or watch the bees pollinate the blossoms. At least sixty shades of green and textures are provided by multiple varieties of hostas, evergreen pine trees, blue spruce bushes, and several types of ornamental grasses. Interspersed throughout, the flowers paint a masterpiece, using an endless pallet of color and texture. We have strawberries and raspberries and blueberries. Little hands tend vegetable gardens. After the children watch the vegetables grow and ripen each week, they can pick and eat them when ready. An arched bridge becomes an awning over a double-sided sand box, and the children can splash and play in a water fountain or listen to it as it trickles musically into the basin. Additionally, an outdoor classroom now provides a place for speech therapy and brain gymnastics exercises.

Nancy told me an interesting story of how she came up with the plan. She had been in the landscape business for over thirty years. When she had a new client, they would have a preliminary meeting and get some parameters for what the client wanted. She would create an initial design and there would be additional meetings to tweak that first design; this process could take several weeks. On a Sunday in 2015, she sat down at her table and started drawing. Within three hours she had the entire garden plan committed to paper. She told me that never once had it happened that quickly. Seemingly without effort, it just flowed out of her. *"Then God said, 'Let the earth bring forth vegetation: every kind of plant that bears seed and every kind of fruit tree on earth that bears fruit with its seed in it.' And so it happened. God saw how good it was."* *(Gen. 1.11-12).*

When new families come into the garden for the first time and get a tour of Reins of Grace, often they will remark about the peaceful feeling they experience when they walk the grounds, but especially in the Sensory Garden. I know it is the Spirit of God that has blessed this farm, this ministry, and Nancy's vision for this "little piece of Heaven.*" "Do not be anxious about anything, but in every situation, by prayer and petition, with thanksgiving, present your requests to God. And the peace of God, which transcends all understanding, will guard your hearts and your minds in Christ Jesus"* *(Phil. 4.6-7).*

Fairy Village

Outdoor Classroom

Walking path through the garden

Goat, not *gold* at end of rainbow

Reins of Grace is a place of hope. God has brought us full circle with the completion of the Sensory Garden. Every individual who rides here is a *whole person*. We address the needs and provide the experiences needed by our riders as they explore and develop their God-given potential. In each stall, coop, field, stone path, or shade tree, the rider and family members will find something delightful and will grow physically, spiritually, and emotionally. Hope lives here.

CHAPTER 18

Where We Are Now...Oops, Wait a Minute

As of August 2019, I thought I had finished this witness and had only a final chapter in which to write a summary of sorts. However, on September 14, 2019, God added one more chapter.

Along with two of my friends, Karen and Tamme, I had planned a trail ride at Tippecanoe State park. We'd been planning it for about six weeks. It was going to take almost two hours to drive there, and we all packed picnic lunches since we planned to spend the whole day riding the trails.

It is important in the therapeutic riding industry to pay attention to the horses' mental and emotional state of mind—some horses more than others. It can be extremely stressful for a therapy horse to do its job. The riders are almost always off balance to some degree, and their weight is constantly being shifted from side to side. Depending on what muscle groups or "weak spots" we are targeting, we change the rider's position on the horse accordingly. A rider can sit on the horse in the traditional forward-facing position, sideways with both legs on one side of the horse, backwards with arms propped on the horses's rump, and even lying down on the horse for a full-body, sensory massage. All these positions can cause stress to the horses's back, shoulders, and haunches.

Additionally, some riders have uncontrollable, loud vocalizations which can startle the horse. Adaptive, modified pieces of equipment are used to support different riders until we can strengthen the riders enough to support themselves.

This is why a therapy horse needs a "vacation" from the arena work and the main reason we go on trail rides—a mental health day for the horses (and humans!)

So here we were, a perfect day weather-wise. Time to saddle up, mount up, and hit the trails.

I climbed up on my little green mounting block—the same one I have used hundreds of times—and swung my right leg over the saddle—the same way I've done it hundreds of times. However, this time, unlike the hundreds of mounts in the past, I must have been standing too close to the edge of the mounting block, and just as I swung my right leg over the saddle, the mounting block tipped over. My right leg stayed stuck on the saddle due to silicone dots on my riding breeches that are designed to keep the rider from sliding around on the slick leather of the saddle. My left leg was on the ground under the horse. All my weight was pulling and stretching the right leg.

At this moment, technically, it would have been within Dundee's rights to spook and jump away because of the sudden slamming of my weight into her rib cage. I had no control over her head. I couldn't pull myself onto the saddle and my silicone breeches wouldn't let me drop to the ground.

Once again, my guardian angels must have been at her head to keep her steady as she simply stepped sideways a few steps to adjust to the sudden weight-shift of my body onto her rib cage. My leg finally came unstuck, and I *gently plopped* to the ground.

When I hit the ground, I said, "Ouch." No scream of pain, no tears, no wailing or clutching my leg, just "ouch."

I quickly self-diagnosed myself with a hyperextension injury. I would need ice, anti-inflammatories, and possibly a knee immobilizer when I got home.

In the meantime, Karen and Tamme helped me to my feet, and I tried to put weight on the right leg, but another "ouch" kept me from putting all my weight on it. I took an Aleve, applied some ice from our coolers to my knee—which was swelling rapidly—and the plan was to wait twenty to thirty minutes for the ice and Aleve to work, and then we would mount up and go riding.

We did not plan this day six weeks in advance, drive two hours and then *not* go trail riding because of a minor knee injury.

Forty minutes later, I talked Karen and Tamme into helping me get on Dundee. For the record, Karen advised against riding, but I was not going to ruin *their* day because of a sprained knee. We all mounted up and started to head out of the parking area when a perfect storm of a truck and trailer, a second truck coming around a corner, and a horse and rider popping out of the bushes at the same time, caused all of our horses to jump and spin.

When Dundee spun around, it caused me to use my right leg and put a lot of weight in the stirrup to brace myself. This time there was a much bigger "ouch," and I realized I would not be able to ride.

We retraced our whopping fifty-foot trail ride back to base camp. Enjoying the beautiful day, we chatted and ate our picnic lunches, but after repeated attempts to use my leg, it became apparent there might be more damage than a sprain. We packed up in order to get back to Indianapolis in time to go to an Urgent Care.

On the way home we tried to come up with a more heroic version of the accident. I was pretty sure I saw a cougar in the trees that was getting ready to pounce on an unsuspecting small child, and by throwing myself between the wild beast and the child, I hurt my leg…

Unfortunately, the truth was that I got "bucked off a mounting block."

At the Urgent Care the attending physician told me I had a fracture of the lateral tibial plateau. A fracture?! It's not as if I was smashed against a tree, fell off a cliff, or a horse rolled on top of me. I *plopped* to the ground—from a *short* pony no less!

Five days later, I had a six-inch plate, nine screws, and an ample amount of bone graft material applied to the right lower extremity—non-weightbearing for a minimum of three months. As I write these words, I am three weeks out from surgery.

I can feel healing taking place every day. Our church community, family and friends are praying, helping take care of the barn and animals, and bringing meals.

It's gray winter now, and as I near the end of my confinement, I can't help but gaze longingly out the window at the Sensory Garden. In 2019, we were able to add an interactive tool and potting shed for the children to plant their own fruits and vegetables. In perfect harmony, everything in the garden feeds the senses—sight, sound, smell, taste, texture, and proprioceptive and vestibular senses.

To boost my spirits and give myself hope, I imagine seeing and smelling the garden coming to life. One of my favorite things is watching the peach tree return from its cold nakedness to the silky, deep green adornment of new leaves with the delicious fragrance of peach blossoms. I will be getting the potting shed ready for tiny hands to sift through warm dirt as they tuck baby seeds into their little brown cradles. The Fairy Garden Village will need to be cleaned out and reorganized. A few winter residents will have to be convinced to find lodging in someone else's garden. When it is warm enough, the children will wash their hair in the slow trickle of the fountain, and then style it with fresh flowers and greenery tucked behind ears. And oh, the decisions! Beans or peas? Cucumbers or squash? Big Boy tomatoes or Cherry tomatoes?

And, of course, we can't forget to plant the carrot box to supply our very talented equine partners with fresh treats all summer long. In just a few short months, our honored, four-legged therapists will soon be back to work for the 2020 riding season at Reins of Grace—Dundee, Sadie, Nellie and Pearlie.

Pearlie...

CHAPTER 19

Pearlie's Story

One of the most fascinating characteristics of a horse is its ability to feel our energy/emotions and *connect* with us. When we experience a range of highs and lows of emotions or feelings, our body chemistry changes. Our temperatures go up or down, our heart rates increase or decrease, our breathing rate also changes. If we are excited or feeling strong, weak, happy, fearful, angry or sad, horses can "understand" those feelings based on our physical changes and our energy. What is most interesting, however, is *they know the difference* between an elevated heart rate due to excitement and joy, or an elevated heart rate due to fear.

Pearlie Queen is one of our Gypsy Vanner horses. She is twenty-years old, and her life's vocation was being a mother. She's had seven beautiful babies, and in fact Nellie is her sixth baby. Eventually, Pearlie was too old to have any more babies, and it was getting more and more difficult to wean her foals. She was so attached and protective of her babies that when it came time to wean one, she would lose over a hundred pounds because she paced the fence line, calling out for her baby and not eating. She would do this for days and days.

When Pearlie first came to Reins of Grace, she was very, very attached to Nellie. It was extremely stressful for her to be separated from Nellie by even a few feet. She was unable to go into the arena by herself because she was so insecure and worried about being separated from Nellie and the other horses. We didn't think she was going to be able to settle down enough to be trained and used for lessons. I started to think about looking for a new home for her.

After my accident in September 2016 (Chapter 1), I was unable to go to the barn for months. Finally, however, I was far enough out from the latest surgery to be able to go see the horses. I still had quite a bit of "apparatus" attached to my leg: wound vac, compression devices, bandages to name a few, but I was determined to get a "horse fix."

I decided to let the horses out for a little exercise. I simply opened Dundee's and Sadie's stall doors, and they went out to the arena. When I got to Pearlie's stall, I knew I needed to put a rope around her neck and lead her out since she wasn't yet trained to go out to the arena on her own. She was still quite nervous anytime we started moving horses around and had a bad habit of dragging people if she couldn't get back to the herd quickly enough.

I put the rope around her neck, opened the door; she nervously and quickly headed for the arena. However, I had seriously underestimated her speed and my ability to keep up with her—even at a walk—and was almost at the point of falling and being dragged, medical appendages and all. I really had no control over her with just a rope around her neck, so all I could do was cry out to her, "Pearlie! Pearlie!" Much to my astonishment, this horse, who only feels comfortable when she is either moving her feet or with a herd, immediately stopped. She then swung her head towards me, ran her nose up and down my injured leg, and froze. She didn't twitch. She didn't look for the other horses. She didn't move an inch. I gathered myself after smoothing down the goosebumps on my arms and asked her to walk on. She did, but her normal walk was too fast for me and I again cried out to her, "Pearlie! Pearlie!" She stopped, still as a stone. For the second time, she swung her head to me, snuffled my injured leg up and down, and waited. A third time, I asked her to walk on, and we *slowly* made it to the gate.

I had goosebumps all over. This was a horse I was sure would never be able to work with our small riders; I couldn't trust her because she was so herd-bound and unconfident. In fact, I had been looking for a new home for her. However, that day I saw her strength and her confidence emerge. She had been a mamma horse all her life, taking care of "little ones," so she recognized the change in my voice. I wasn't the "alpha Julie" she knew. I was "fragile Julie,"—she heard it in my voice and took care of me.

That was the beginning of hope. I was now somewhat sure that Pearlie could be trained to give lessons to our small riders. We just needed to tap into her strength—being a mom. In the spring of 2017, this seedling of a thought grew and blossomed.

I received a phone call one day from a family who had a son on the autism spectrum. They were interested in signing up for lessons. Before lessons begin, I like to have the whole family come out to take a tour of Reins of Grace, meet all the horses, goats, and chickens, and allow the kids to explore with "no pressure." When transitioning to a new routine, a child with ASD (Autism Spectrum Disorder) can find change very disruptive; this, of course, affects parents as well. Exploring Reins of Grace makes initiating lessons much easier for the entire family.

On the day Zach and his family came out, we started our tour by going from stall to stall to meet the horses. It was quite a large group: mom and dad, four small siblings, an aunt and uncle—and, of course, Zach. We started with Dundee. I opened the stall door just enough for Dundee to poke her head out and accept a treat from me, allowing the family to observe her while I gave them a little information. We next moved on to Sadie's stall and repeated the process. Zach was feeling a little overwhelmed and was glued to his dad's hip; he hadn't said a word.

After introducing Sadie, we moved to Pearlie's stall. As I started to slide her door open just enough for her to get her head through, she immediately shoved her head against the door to open it wider, took two steps out of her stall, then stopped. She looked at this crowd of people very intently;

she then slowly and carefully stretched out her neck and head, past three other small children and the adults, to gently touch Zach with her nose. He was wide-eyed and seemed very nervous, but he didn't move.

Pearlie then started to snuffle him from head to toe, starting with his cheek and moving down to his shoe. *We were all astounded.* No one said a word. Even his parents, who "didn't know horses," knew something amazing had just occurred. *I knew horses—and Pearlie—I was speechless.* We were all rooted to our spots as we watched this mother horse seek out and comfort the one child in this crowd of people who was "fragile." Pearlie knew who needed her. This was her "baby." As she stood quietly, she softly licked her lips and let out a contented sigh.

Pearlie had her new job and her purpose. She was going to do what she knew best—serve as a mother to all our fragile little ones who come to ride at Reins of Grace.

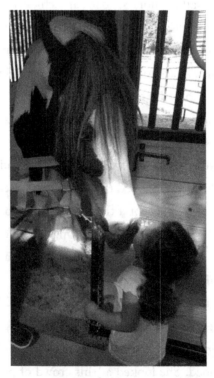

Pearlie Love

CHAPTER 20

Finally

I am trying to discern all the positives that God intends to accomplish through this latest medical challenge. Included are such things as patience and giving up control, as well as humility and more reliance on Him. Through these physical trials, He has deepened my understanding and empathy for the families we serve. *"Because he himself was tested through what he suffered he is able to help those who are being tested"* *(Heb. 2.18)*

As I mentioned earlier in Chapter One, I think God wanted me to use my three months of non-weightbearing confinement time wisely and finish the story of Reins of Grace. Occasionally in the past, I have given talks about Reins of Grace at various schools, churches, and community centers. When I heard myself speaking, I realized it was not a "book" God wanted me to write, but rather a witness of God's great desire to be part of our *daily* lives—demonstrated by how He guided my life and ministry, one breadcrumb at a time.

You don't have to be an "important somebody" to know God and have a personal relationship with Him. I am, theologically speaking and otherwise, a nobody. Just an average Joe. A sinner, selfish. ***"For all have sinned and come short of the glory of God" (Rom. 3.23).***

Thankfully and mercifully, God sent his only son, Jesus Christ, to save us. ***"For God so loved the world that he gave his only Son, so that everyone who believes in him might not perish but might have eternal life"(John 3.16).***

He wants a relationship with *you*. Even though you may not realize it, He is guiding you with breadcrumbs that belong to you alone. God is wholeheartedly invested in pursuing you; He desires to commune with you. When you yearn for that intimacy, He will never give you half-hearted, sporadic attention. God wants more, *we need more*. Our God is not a remote, sitting-on-a-tall-distant-mountain God. He is an interactive, hands-on, fully present, loving God. *It really is that simple.* ***"For you formed my inward parts; you knitted me together in my mother's womb. I praise you, for I am fearfully and wonderfully made. Wonderful are your works; my soul knows it very well. My frame was not hidden from you, when I was being made in secret, intricately woven in the depths of the earth. Your eyes saw my unformed substance; in your book were written, every one of them, the days that were formed for me, when as yet there was none of them" (Psal.139.12-16).***

What you may think is an "insignificant" matter that would be a "bother" to God is, in fact, never trivial to Him. All the incidents in this book are real and most assuredly *not* coincidences.

I guess that is the point of writing this all down. If you are trying to discern the possibility of taking a "leap of faith," whether it is a new business, a personal commitment, a defining of boundaries—anything that is fraught with self-doubt, lack of confidence, lack of financial resources—just look at how God literally directed my path step by step, one breadcrumb at a time. He wants to help all of us on our journey to being with Him for Eternity.

I use the term "discernment," a complicated and somewhat nebulous process for me. When other people would tell me to pray and *discern* God's will, I didn't know how to do it or what to expect. Is He going to talk to me audibly, will He do a writing on the wall? Some kind of memo? A prophetic dream or vision? *"But if any of you lacks wisdom, he should ask God who gives to all generously and ungrudgingly, and he will be given it. But he should ask in faith, not doubting..." (Jas. 1.5,6.)*

My sophisticated discernment in this journey was to simply take the next step I *thought* God was asking of me, knowing that if I took the wrong step, He would *shut it down*. That is how I knew I was following His will. However, I had to make that phone call, take that step, make a financial commitment *first* and rely on God to show me unequivocally if I was on the right track. *"Have I not commanded you? Be strong and courageous. Do not be frightened, and do not be dismayed, for the Lord your God is with you wherever you go" (Josh. 1.9).*

As I recover from this latest physical challenge, I am keeping my mind and heart open to where He is leading me and how He wants me to use this experience to benefit and encourage others. When the next breadcrumb from heaven calls, I will try not to "horse around" but hear and follow His path, wherever it may lead. *"Fear not, for I am with you; be not dismayed, for I am your God; I will strengthen you, I will help you, I will uphold you with my righteous right hand" (Isa. 41.10).*

La Paloma's Legacy

Printed in the United States
By Bookmasters